To Levi, Vivienne, Remy, Magnolia, Charlie, Piper, Seamus, Ethan, Graham, Vivian and every other child who enjoys tiny dinosaurs

With gratitude for the
advice and contributions of
Michael Matheron

by Susan Meadows
November 2022

ISBN   979-8-9874717-0-8

Counting Tiny Dinosaurs

0

Zero tiny dinosaurs.

1

One tiny dinosaur.

2

1, 2

Two tiny dinosaurs.

3

1, 2, 3

Three tiny dinosaurs.

4

1, 2, 3, 4

Four tiny dinosaurs.

5

1, 2, 3, 4, 5

Five tiny dinosaurs.

6

1, 2, 3, 4, 5, 6

Six tiny dinosaurs.

7

1, 2, 3, 4, 5, 6, 7

Seven tiny dinosaurs.

8

1, 2, 3, 4, 5, 6, 7, 8

Eight tiny dinosaurs.

9

1, 2, 3, 4, 5, 6, 7, 8, 9

Nine tiny dinosaurs.

10

1, 2, 3, 4, 5, 6, 7, 8, 9, 10

Ten tiny dinosaurs.

11

1, 2, 3, 4, 5, 6, 7, 8, 9, 10, 11

Eleven tiny dinosaurs.

12

1, 2, 3, 4, 5, 6, 7, 8, 9, 10, 11, 12

Twelve tiny dinosaurs.

Many

Many tiny dinosaurs, more than twelve.

Why Tiny Dinosaurs?

You may ask why birds in this book are counted as tiny dinosaurs. There are several reasons. Mostly, it is because birds are descendants of the dinosaurs known now as theropods. Theropods include the velociraptors and the ferocious Tyrannosaurus rex.

Birds evolved over enormous expanses of time. First came the bipedalism of the theropods, then feathers. Some feathered bipedal dinosaurs eventually evolved into increasingly small creatures unlike their more typical dinosaur cousins who grew larger. Their bones became hollow. In the last, birds evolved true wings and the great differentiator, beaks. They could fly and collect food.

When the dinosaurs became extinct some ancient birds were living among them. One ancient bird that survives in modern times is the emu.

Another reason for using "tiny dinosaurs" is that children typically love dinosaurs. To see in the birds around them their dinosaur origins is a great treat.

I hope you and the children with whom you share this book enjoy the concept and counting tiny dinosaurs wherever you are.

Source *How Dinosaurs Shrank and Became Birds* by Emily Singer, Quanta Magazine on June 12, 2015

www.ingramcontent.com/pod-product-compliance
Lightning Source LLC
Chambersburg PA
CBHW060839270326
41933CB00002B/135